My journal about Me!

a keepsake celebrating the "me-ness" of me

My journal about Me!

This journal is part of the *Hooray for You!*
product collection, inspired by the well-loved gift book,
Hooray for You!, a celebration of "you-ness,"
written and illustrated by Marianne Richmond.

Marianne Richmond Studios, Inc.
420 N. 5th Street, Suite 840
Minneapolis, MN 55401
www.mariannerichmond.com

ISBN 0-9652448-9-X

Text and illustrations by Marianne Richmond

Book design by Meg Anderson

Printed in China

Second Printing

I started it on

this day _____

in the year of _____

in the city of _____

when I was in this grade _____

and was _____ years old.

I finished it on

this day _____

in the year of _____

in the city of _____

when I was in this grade _____

and was _____ years old.

It was given to me by

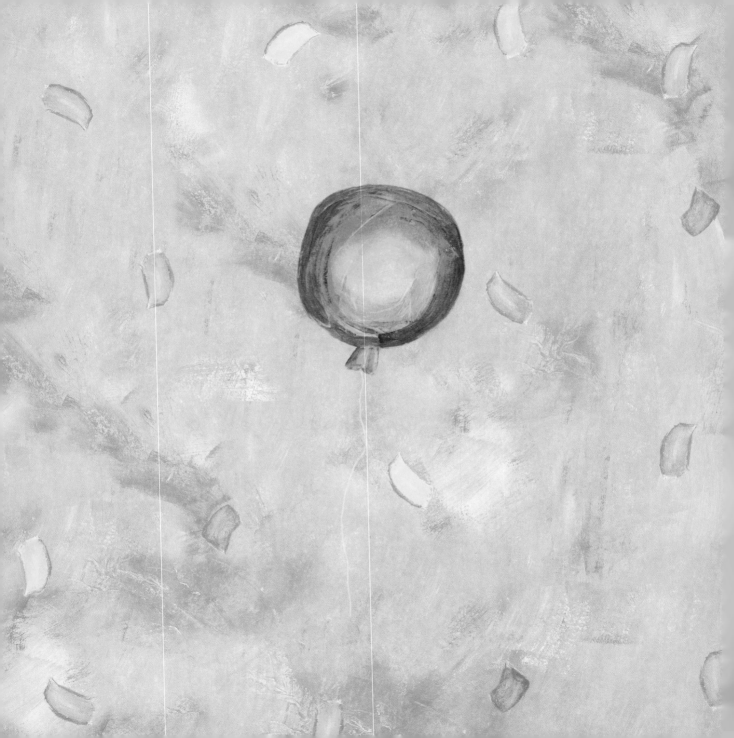

About this journal

Hello! We created this journal because YOU are the only YOU in this whole wide world! No one shares your exact thoughts, feelings, likes, dislikes, and general "take on life." We wanted to give you a fun book in which you can record, vent, draw, be silly or secretive... and perhaps learn something about yourself along the way!

Journaling is a wonderful way to tap into your creativity, take stock of your gifts, let go of something bugging you, or explore an idea. The best part of all? You can do this journal at your pace, when the writing mood strikes. Answer one question or several. Skip around. Answer the same question two years in a row. Be sure to date your entries so you can see how your feelings change as you grow. And most of all—

Have fun!!

Write your full name. What do you like best about your name? If you could change your name, what new name would you choose?

Are you named after someone special?
(parent, grandparent, etc.)

Describe what you look like.

(short, tall, blue eyes, curly hair, etc.)

date..

Include a **favorite picture** of yourself here.

Me!

....**date**

List ten things (or more!) you **like most** about yourself.

1.

2.

3.

4.

5.

6.

7.

8.

9.

10.

date ....

If you could **change** one thing about yourself ...

what would it be and why?

Pretend you are listening to a conversation about you. How would you **like** to hear people **describing you** to others? (nice, funny, friendly, smart, pretty, handsome, honest, etc.)

date ....

When is your **birthday?** Do you think this is a **good time** of **year** to have a birthday?

Describe a **favorite** way you have celebrated a **birthday.** Describe a **favorite gift** you have received.

Where do you live (street, city, state)? Include a picture of your house here. What do you **like best** about your **home?**

Include a picture of your **bedroom** here. Is it usually messy or clean? Do you have your own room or do you **share** it? What do you **like to do** when you hang out in your room? What are the **favorite** things you keep here?

Name all the people in your life who love you for just being you.

"If people compare you with another,
like a mother or sister or uncle or brother
To them you can say for certain indeed,
"I'm completely for sure
ME guaranteed!"

family reunion

Write about your **family.** Do you have brothers or sisters?
If yes, are you the oldest, youngest or in between?

Who do people say you **look like?** Do you agree or disagree?

....**date**

Include some **pictures** of your family here.

date ....

Describe your parents.

....date

What do you like to do together?

date..

Recall a happy memory of your **grandparents** if you can. If not, ask your mom or dad to tell you a story about your grandma or grandpa. Include a picture of your grandparents here.

Describe some of the **fun things** your family does together.

date..

What **chores** are you responsible for in your house? Do you get an **allowance** for your contribution?

Describe the **best family vacation** you've had. If you could plan the **next** one, where would you go and why?

date..

Is there anything about your family that **bugs** you?

What is it?

Does your family own or have they ever owned a **pet?** If so, write about this **special member** of your family. Include a picture of your pet here.

Friends

date...

Write about your **friends.** Do you have one **best friend?**
Several close friends? List your friends' names here.

Do you have any **far away** friends? Do you write letters or
e-mail to each other?

What is important to you **in a friend?**

date..

What activities do you and your **friends** like to do together?

What do you and your **friends** talk about? What **secrets** have you shared **with your friends?**

date..

Has a friend ever **hurt** your **feelings?** How did you
resolve your **conflict?** Have you ever done or said
something to a friend that you **regret?** Did you apologize?

....date

Paste pictures here of your **friends.**

My Friends!

date...

Describe your **special skills** and **talents**.

Describe some **accomplishments** you are really **proud** of.

How do you see yourself as a grown up? Do you want to be single? Married? Do you want kids?

If you could live in any part of the world you wanted ... where would you pick and why?

List some things you want to **learn more** about ... or become better at .... in the coming months and years.

date..

Create a **"dream collage"** with pictures, drawings, and words that reflect your heart's desires.

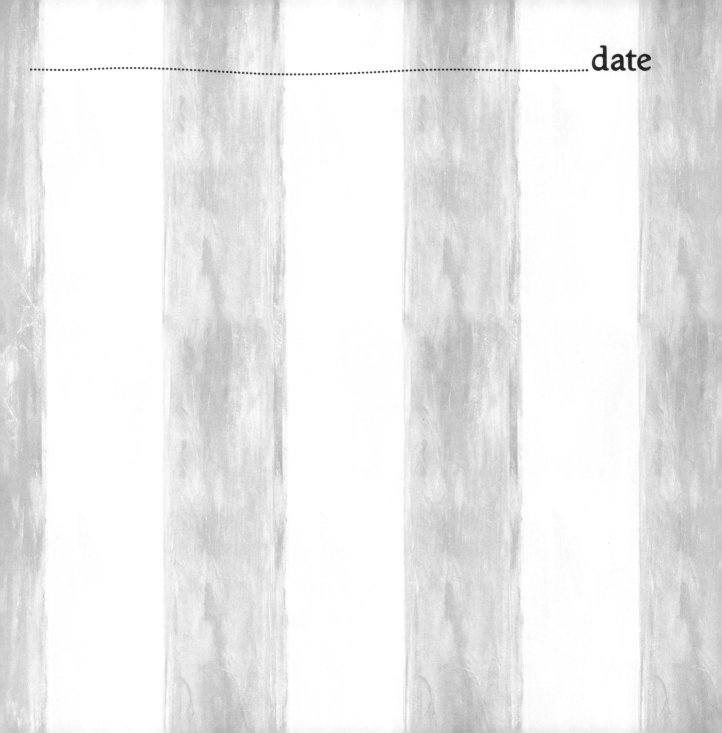

date

date ....

What do you **daydream** about?

Write a **poem or short story** about someone or something **important** to you. Include illustrations if you'd like.

date..

What kinds of **things** do you **think about** right before you fall asleep at night?

If you could **meet any person** from history, **who** would it be and **why?**

If you won the **lottery,** what would you do with your **millions** of dollars?

Pretend you are able to instantly make **three wishes** come true. What would you wish for and why?

1.

2.

3.

Is **prayer** part of your life? If so, what kind of things do you
pray about?

date ....

Thoughts 'n doodles

....date

Thoughts 'n doodles

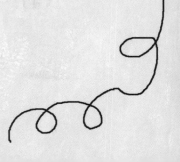

My **feelings** deep down...

date...

What makes you **happy?**

And **sad?**

Describe a time you felt **scared**.

or **nervous.**

date..

Draw the **feelings** in your **heart** today.

List several things for which you feel **grateful.**

"There are foods you find yummy.
A **favorite** color or two.
Things you don't like ...
but more that you do!"

date..

What is your **favorite** ...

color?

food?

ice cream flavor?

candy / snack?

....**date**

Write about your **favorite books, TV shows, movies,** and **music** ...

date ....

What is your **favorite sport** to watch?

To **play?**

What is your **favorite clothing** to wear?

Why do you like it?

date..

What is your **favorite** thing to do **after school?**

How about on the **weekends?**

.... **date**

Do you have a **favorite day** of the week? What is it and **why?**

Saturday 1

Friday

Thursday

8

7

15

6

14

5

13

21

date..

Do you have a **hobby?** If yes, describe **what it is** and
why you like it.

Who is / was your **favorite teacher** in school? What makes him/her so special?

Have **you** ever been a **teacher** to someone else?

What did you teach them?

What is your **favorite subject** in school? Your **least favorite?**

Is there a **person** in your life that you **admire?** If yes, what is it about him/her that you especially like?

....date